Robots

by
David Orme

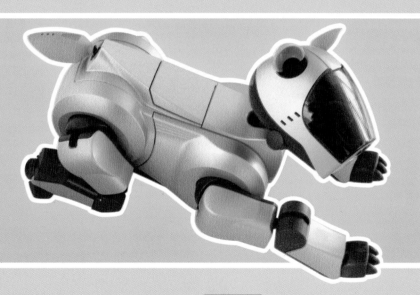

Thunderbolts

Robots
by David Orme

Illustrated by Mark Draisey

Published by Ransom Publishing Ltd.
Radley House, 8 St. Cross Road, Winchester, Hants. SO23 9HX, UK
www.ransom.co.uk

ISBN   978 178127 081 3

First published in 2013

Contents

THUNDER BOLTS

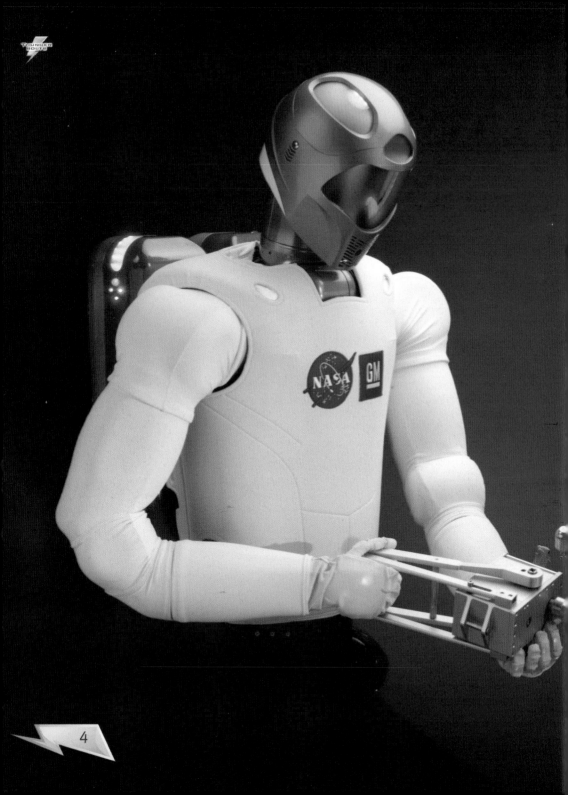

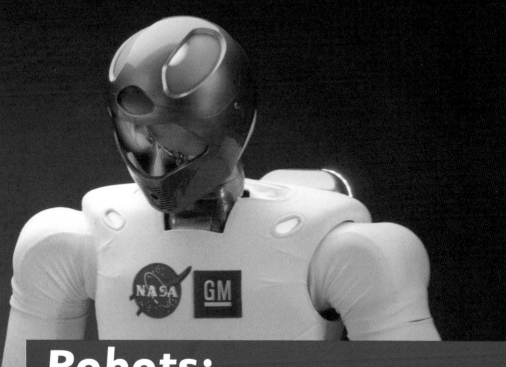

Robots:
The Facts

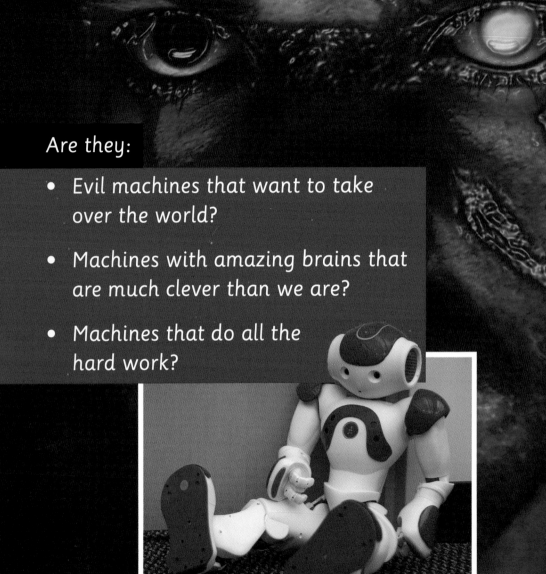

Are they:

- Evil machines that want to take over the world?

- Machines with amazing brains that are much clever than we are?

- Machines that do all the hard work?

6

A robot that does all the housework would be great.

But what if it decided that it didn't want to work any more?

An ancient robot

Robots aren't new.

This is a model of a robot built by Leonardo da Vinci in 1495.

What could it do? It could sit, stand and wave its arms about. It could open and close its mouth.

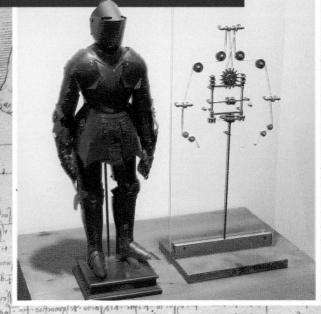

A robot on Mars.

Some of Leonardo's ideas were so good they are being used now.

They have helped to design robots for space stations.

These robots may even help to explore Mars!

Robots at home

Would you like a robot in your house?

Well, you have! Lots of them!

Here are some of the robots in your house.

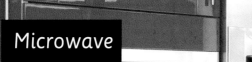
Microwave

'Fridge

Cooker

Washing machine

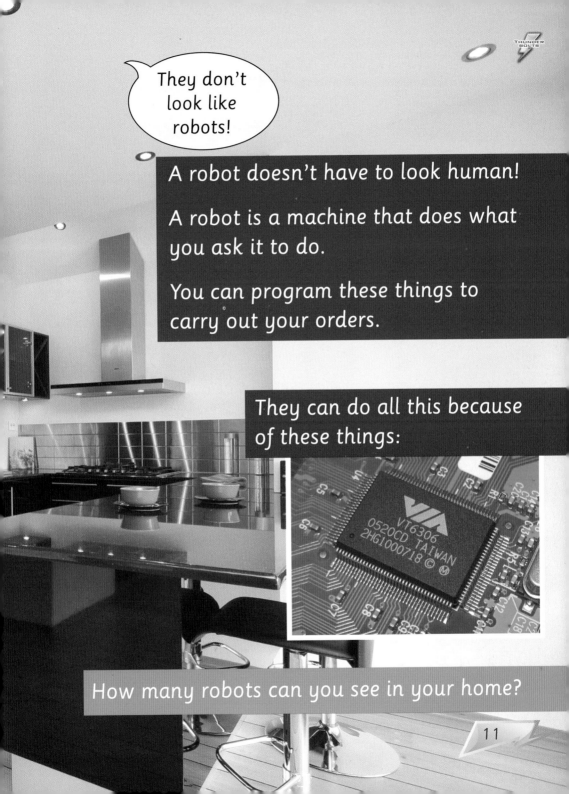

They don't look like robots!

A robot doesn't have to look human!

A robot is a machine that does what you ask it to do.

You can program these things to carry out your orders.

They can do all this because of these things:

How many robots can you see in your home?

Factory robots

Here is a factory making cars a long time ago.

This is a car factory today.

Now factories are full of robots instead of people!

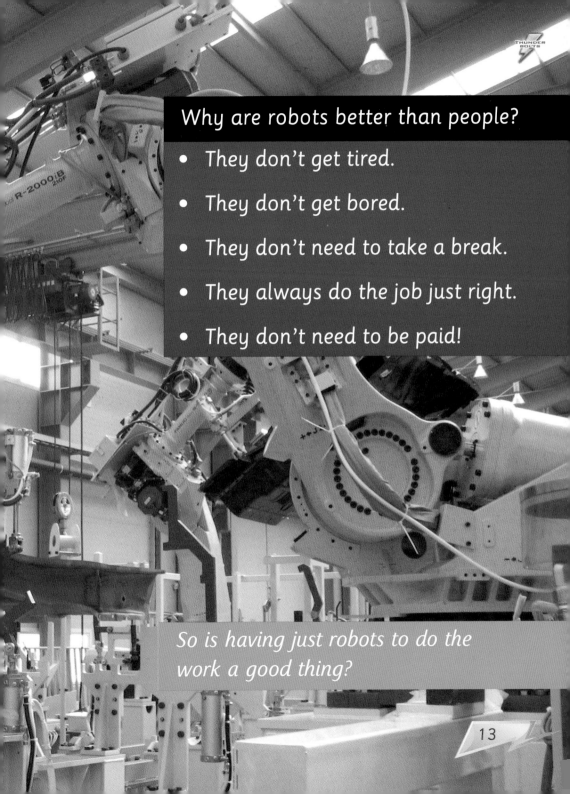

Why are robots better than people?

- They don't get tired.

- They don't get bored.

- They don't need to take a break.

- They always do the job just right.

- They don't need to be paid!

So is having just robots to do the work a good thing?

ASIMO the robot

This is ASIMO. ASIMO is an amazing walking robot.

What can ASIMO do?

- It can walk without bumping into things, and go up and down stairs.

- It can recognise people by their faces and speak to them.

- It can carry out instructions.

- It knows when its battery is low and can recharge itself.

- It can even play football!

In the future, robots like ASIMO could help people who find it hard to walk or do jobs at home.

Underwater robots

The bottom of the ocean is a dangerous place to work and explore.

What's the answer?

Let robots do it!

They can:

- Explore the deepest parts of the sea and send back pictures and information

- Check for pollution in the sea

- Mend underwater pipes and cables

- Explore old wrecks – and maybe even find treasure!

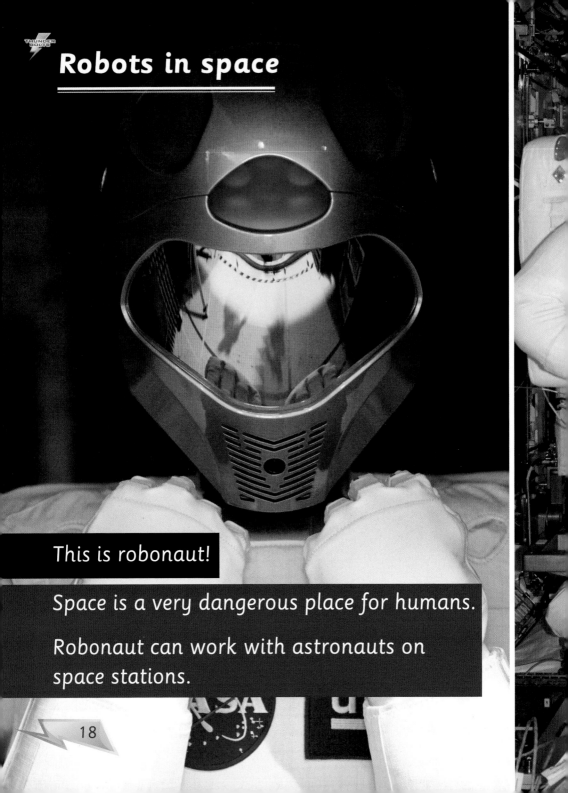

Robots in space

This is robonaut!

Space is a very dangerous place for humans.

Robonaut can work with astronauts on space stations.

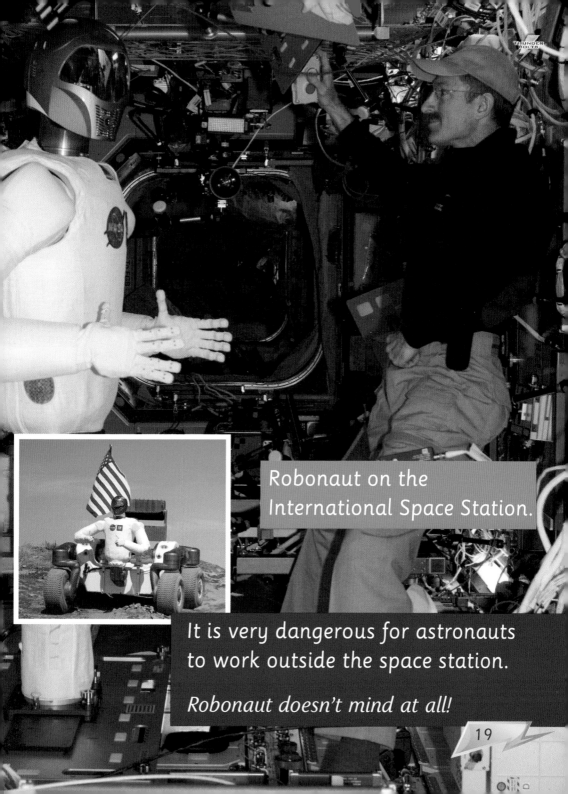

Robonaut on the International Space Station.

It is very dangerous for astronauts to work outside the space station.

Robonaut doesn't mind at all!

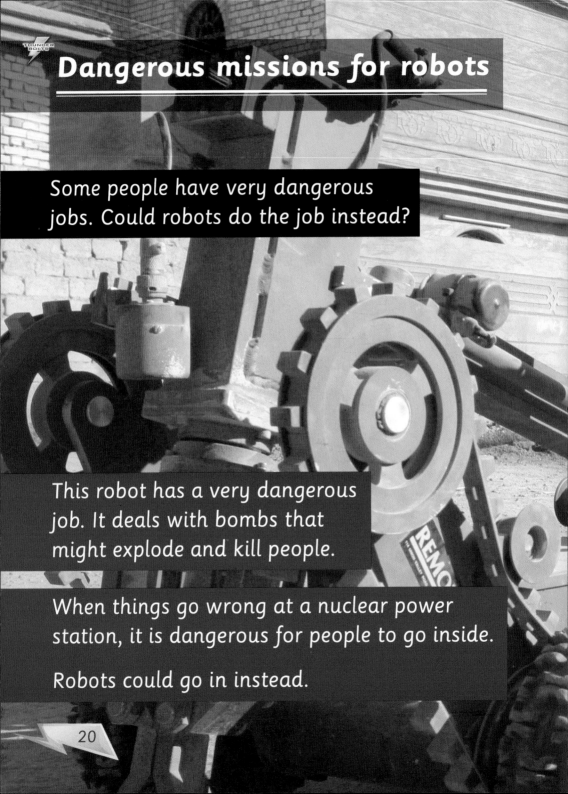

Dangerous missions for robots

Some people have very dangerous jobs. Could robots do the job instead?

This robot has a very dangerous job. It deals with bombs that might explode and kill people.

When things go wrong at a nuclear power station, it is dangerous for people to go inside.

Robots could go in instead.

In the future, robots could:

- fight fires

- fight wars as soldiers.

Some people think this is a really bad idea.

Do you agree?

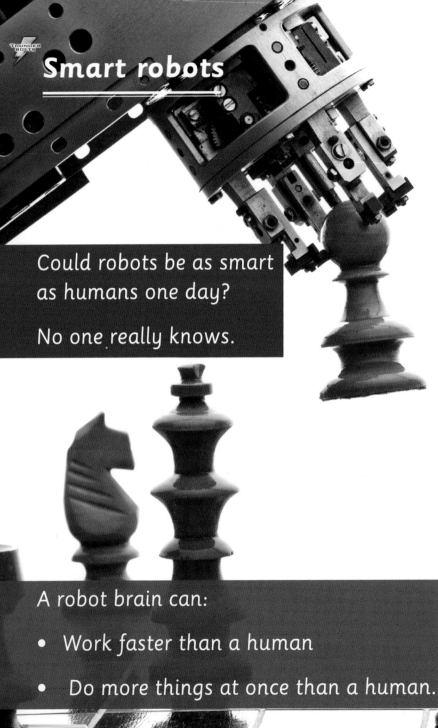

Smart robots

Could robots be as smart as humans one day?

No one really knows.

A robot brain can:

- Work faster than a human

- Do more things at once than a human.

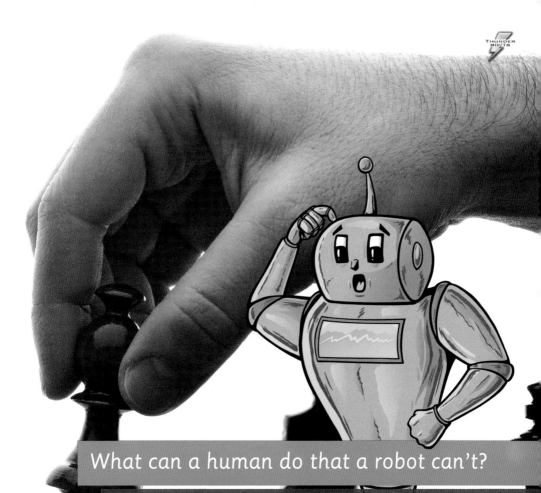

What can a human do that a robot can't?

Humans can:

- Use what happens to them to help them change the way they think

- Use imagination to invent things, or write poems or music

- Enjoy things

- Understand jokes!

23

This family has ordered a robot to do the housework.

Dad can't understand the instructions, but Sam and Lisa can!

The robot is ready to go – but first they need to charge the battery.

The robot is brilliant.

It gets all the jobs done – and it never gets tired.

The family think it's great!

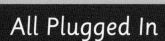

It's the middle of the night, and the family are all in bed.

Now who forgot to unplug the robot?

What's going to happen in the morning?

Looks like the family is doing all the work again! They really should have unplugged that robot!

The robot makes a call – to invite all his robot friends round.

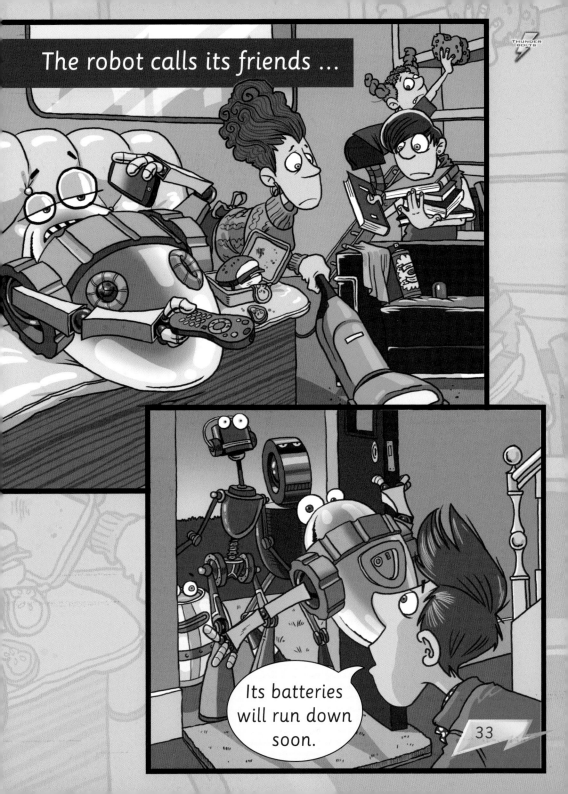

The family are tired out. They are off to bed.

Dad thinks everything will be OK when the robot's batteries run down.

But is he right?

The family are tired out!

Don't forget to plug yourselves in, guys!

Word list

ancient	International Space Station
ASIMO	
astronaut	Leonardo da Vinci
battery	machine
charge	microwave
dangerous	mission
evil	nuclear
factory	pollution
housework	recharge
human	robonaut
imagination	space station
information	treasure
instructions	